PRAISE FOR
Building a Bridge

"A welcome and much-needed book that will help bishops, priests, pastoral associates, and all church leaders more compassionately minister to the LGBT community. It will also help LGBT Catholics feel more at home in what is, after all, their church."

—Cardinal Kevin Farrell, Prefect of the Vatican's
Dicastery for Laity, Family, and Life

"Sexuality, gender, and religion—a volatile mix. With this book, Father Martin shows how the Rosary and the rainbow flag can peacefully meet each other. After this must-read you will understand why New Ways Ministry honored Father Martin with its Bridge Building Award."

—Sister Jeannine Gramick, SL, cofounder of New
Ways Ministry and longtime LGBT advocate

"The Gospel demands that LGBT Catholics must be genuinely loved and treasured in the life of the church. They are not. In *Building a Bridge,* James Martin provides us with the language, perspective, and sense of urgency to undertake the arduous but monumentally Christlike task of replacing a culture of alienation with a culture of encounter and merciful inclusion."

—Robert W. McElroy, Bishop of San Diego

"If you think a call to build bridges is a letdown because you wanted some more confrontational form of resistance, don't be fooled: being a peacemaker in this field is delicate and costly, and Father Martin, who has been building such bridges for many years, packs more of a punch than appears at first reading. He, like Pope Francis, knows that it is by drawing dangerously close and entering into relationships that we learn mercy, equality of heart, and love of enemies. If, and only if, we can be Christian in those things, then the scandal at the heart of the relationship between LGBT believers and our churches is well on the way to being undone."

—James Alison, author of *Faith Beyond Resentment: Fragments Gay and Catholic*

"In too many parts of our church LGBT people have been made to feel unwelcome, excluded, and even shamed. Father Martin's brave, prophetic, and inspiring book marks an essential step in inviting church leaders to minister with more compassion and in reminding LGBT Catholics that they are as much a part of our church as any other Catholic."

—Cardinal Joseph Tobin, Archbishop of Newark

Building a Bridge

How the Catholic Church and the
LGBT Community Can Enter
into a Relationship of Respect,
Compassion, and Sensitivity

JAMES MARTIN, SJ

HarperOne
An Imprint of HarperCollins*Publishers*

Imprimi Potest: Very Rev. John Cecero, SJ, Provincial Superior, USA Northeast Province of the Society of Jesus.

FIRST EDITION

Designed by SBI Book Arts, LLC

Library of Congress Cataloging-in-Publication Data has been applied for.

ISBN 978-0-06-269431-7

17 18 19 20 21   LSC   10 9 8 7 6 5 4 3 2 1

Dedicated to all the LGBT people
and their families and friends
who have shared their joys and hopes
and their griefs and anxieties with me

For it was you who formed
my inward parts;

you knit me together in
my mother's womb.

I praise you, for I am fearfully
and wonderfully made.

Wonderful are your works;

that I know very well.

PSALM 139:13–14

CONTENTS

Why I'm Writing

In the summer of 2016, a gunman stormed into a nightclub popular among the gay community in Orlando, Florida, and killed forty-nine people. It was, at that time, the largest mass shooting in U.S. history.

In response, millions in this country grieved and voiced their support for the LGBT (lesbian, gay, bisexual, and transgender) community. But I was concerned by what I did not hear. Although many church leaders expressed both sorrow and horror, only a handful of the more than 250 Catholic bishops used the words *gay* or *LGBT*. Cardinal Blase Cupich, of Chicago; Bishop Robert Lynch, of St. Petersburg, Florida; Bishop David Zubik, of Pittsburgh; Bishop Robert McElroy, of San Diego; and Bishop John Stowe, of Lexington, Kentucky, all spoke out strongly in support of the LGBT community and against homophobia. Many, however, remained silent.

I found this revelatory. The fact that only a few Catholic bishops acknowledged the LGBT community or even used the word *gay* at such a time showed that the LGBT community is still invisible in many quarters of the church. Even in tragedy its members are invisible.

This event helped me to recognize something in a new way: the work of the Gospel cannot be accomplished if one part of the church is essentially separated from any other part. Between the two groups, the LGBT community and the institutional church, a chasm has formed, a separation for which a bridge needs to be built.

For many years, I've ministered to and worked with LGBT people, most of them Catholics. My ministry has not been primarily through classes or seminars, but rather through more informal channels. Gay, lesbian, bisexual, and transgender people as well as their parents and friends have come to me for advice, counsel, confession, and spiritual direction. After Masses, lectures, or retreats, they will ask advice on spiritual and religious matters, pose questions on church-related issues, or simply share their experiences.

During these times, I've listened to their joys and hopes, their griefs and anxieties, sometimes accompanied by tears, sometimes by laughter. In the process, I've become friends with many of them. Most priests, deacons, sisters, brothers, and lay pastoral workers in the church could probably say the same thing.

I've also worked with and come to know many cardinals, archbishops, bishops, and other church officials and leaders. After thirty years as a Jesuit and twenty years working for a Catholic media ministry, I've come to know members of the hierarchy through a variety of ways, from speaking events to dinner-table conversations. I've become friends with many church leaders, and I rely on their wise counsel and pastoral support.

Over the years, then, I've discovered a great divide. I lament that there isn't more understanding and conversation between LGBT Catholics and the institutional church. I would rather not refer to two "sides," since everyone is part of the church. But many LGBT Catholics have told me that they have felt hurt by the institutional church—unwelcomed, excluded, and insulted. At the same time, many in the institutional church want to reach out to this community, but seem somewhat confused about how to do so. Yes, I know it seems that there are some who don't seem to want to reach out, but all the bishops I know are sincere in their desire for true pastoral outreach.

For the past three decades as a Jesuit, part of my ministry has been, informally, trying to build bridges between these groups. But after the shooting in Orlando, my desire to do so intensified.

So when New Ways Ministry, a group that ministers to and advocates for LGBT Catholics, asked just a few weeks after the Orlando tragedy if I would accept their "Bridge Building Award" and give a talk at the time of the award ceremony, I agreed. The name of the award, as it turned out, inspired me to sketch out an idea for a "two-way bridge" that might help bring together both the institutional church and the LGBT community.

The bulk of this book is that talk, which has been expanded into a longer essay. The essay urges the church to treat the LGBT community with "respect, compassion, and sensitivity" (a phrase from the *Catechism of the Catholic Church*) and the LGBT community to reciprocate, reflecting those virtues in its own relationship with the institutional church.

Let me say something important at the outset. I understand the difficulties that many LGBT people have faced in the church. They have shared stories with me about being insulted, slandered, excluded, rejected, and even fired. I don't want to minimize that pain. Still, I believe it's important for the LGBT community, for everyone in fact, to treat others with respect, even when their own church at times feels like an enemy. That is part of being a Christian, hard as it is.

This does not mean that one cannot critique and challenge the church when it needs to be critiqued and challenged. But all of that can be done with "respect, compassion, and sensitivity." In fact, respect, compassion, and sensitivity are undervalued gifts for dealing with conflict and disagreement in general, gifts that can be shared with the wider culture. These virtues can help not only Catholics and Christians, but all people of goodwill who seek unity.

In recent years, in fact, the overall social and political climate in the United States has become more divisive and social discourse more contentious. Even abroad, various social, political, and ethnic groups find themselves pitted against one another with an intensity that seems not only new, but frightening. Not too long ago, opposing factions would often interact with one another politely and work together for the common good. Certainly there were tensions, but a kind of quiet courtesy and tacit respect prevailed. Now all one seems to find is contempt. As a result, many people feel powerless to prevent the continued fraying of the social fabric as well as the name-calling, personal attacks, and violence that such division gives rise to.

For me, the "echo chambers" created by social media in which one's worldview is barely challenged, news channels specializing in simplistic and sometimes false analyses of complicated political situations, and civic leaders seemingly unconcerned about the division that their words and actions might cause are all developments that contribute to this disunity, as well as to the feelings of hopelessness that arise in the face of this disunity.

In these times, the church should be a sign of unity. Frankly, in all times. Yet many people see the church as contributing to division, as some Christian leaders and their congregations mark off boundaries of "us" and "them." But the church works best when it embodies the virtues of respect, compassion, and sensitivity.

So I hope that this brief book might be a meditation for the church at large, not simply for those interested in LGBT issues.

A few notes. First of all, not every church leader needs to be upbraided for not treating LGBT Catholics with care. Far from it. Besides the bishops I mentioned above, there are dozens more, at least in the United States, who are warm and welcoming to the LGBT community, and there are many American parishes with vibrant outreach programs to this community. Many bishops and priests—to say nothing of deacons, sisters and brothers, and Catholic lay leaders—should be praised. In fact, one of the surprising aspects of the church for non-Catholics is how much ministry to the LGBT community goes on, in quiet and unheralded ways, in so many dioceses and parishes.

Second, not every LGBT person struggles with self-acceptance; these days the process of coming to understand one's identity as an LGBT person is easier than it was just a few decades ago.

One of the most moving parts for me of the gathering at New Ways Ministry in Baltimore was being accompanied by two friends: one a young man, age sixteen, who had just admitted being gay to his classmates at a Catholic high school; and the other his father, in his late forties, who had accepted his son with open arms and an open heart. And the very next weekend, on a trip to Philadelphia for a parish talk, I was given a ride from the train station by two brothers, both in their twenties. One of them, a college student, spontaneously told me that he was gay, in a relaxed manner that quickly telegraphed his complete comfort with his sexuality.

So I don't wish to imply by some of my comments, or the biblical passages appearing in this book, that an LGBT person *should* feel excluded. Some LGBT people simply presume, as they should, their place in the church and aren't much bothered by the stray negative comments they hear. For most LGBT people at any age, however, the process of understanding that they are loved by God as they are and the process of finding their place in the church remain difficult ones.

By the way, my use of *LGBT* as an adjective is not meant to exclude anyone; this is the most common nomenclature at the time that I'm writing. One could also use LGBTQ (lesbian, gay, bisexual, transgender, and questioning or queer) or LGBTQA (lesbian, gay, bisexual, transgender, questioning or queer, and allies) or

LGBT+. Perhaps someday we might settle on a shorter acronym or inclusive name, but my goal is to include all people who may feel that their spiritual journey and their welcome in the church have been made more difficult by their sexual orientation.

Overall, I'd like to offer a bridge for all of us, and then offer further support for that bridge by providing something I've hoped to share in print for some time: a series of biblical passages that have proven helpful for LGBT Catholics as well as brief reflections on those passages. Some of them are mentioned in the text of the essay—like the stories of Jesus's healing of the Roman centurion's servant and Jesus's encounter with Zacchaeus. At first blush, you might wonder what these familiar passages could possibly say to LGBT people, but when you see the story through new eyes, I hope it will become obvious.

I have also included other biblical passages that have, based on my experience in ministry, proven the most helpful in the spiritual journeys of LGBT Catholics. These too will be accompanied by brief reflections and questions as an aid to praying with those passages.

These select biblical passages and my own reflections are also meant for LGBT allies, parents, friends, and the entire church—including parishes and dioceses, priests and bishops. The Bible, after all, is for everyone. I hope that my reflections might be of help on both the personal level and the communal level, to invite parishes and dioceses into communal prayer, conversation, discernment, and action.

Finally, I know this topic—the treatment of LGBT people in the church and the church's outreach to them—is a highly sensitive subject for many people. Because I have met and ministered to many LGBT people, I know that each situation is unique and that many of those situations are imbued with great anguish. So I apologize if any feel I am minimizing their pain, misunderstanding their situation, needlessly scolding them, or leaving out something important. My experience with LGBT people is lengthy, but it is certainly not as extensive as that of others who work in this ministry directly.

This essay, then, is not a complete road map, but rather a starting point, an occasion for reflection and conversation. Feel free to disagree. Please reflect on what you find helpful in this book and leave the rest behind.

So my brothers and sisters, I invite you to join me on a bridge.

A Two-Way Bridge

The relationship between LGBT Catholics and the Catholic Church has been at times contentious and combative and at times warm and welcoming. Much of the tension characterizing this complicated relationship results, I believe, from a lack of communication and a good deal of mistrust between LGBT Catholics and the hierarchy. What is needed is a bridge between that community and the church.

So I would like to invite you to walk with me as I describe how we might build that bridge. To that end, I would like to reflect on both the church's outreach to the LGBT community and the LGBT community's outreach to the church, because good bridges take people in both directions.

As you probably know, the *Catechism of the Catholic Church* says that Catholics are called to treat homosexuals with "respect, compassion, and sensitivity" (No. 2358).

What might that mean? Let's meditate on that question, and on a second question as well: what might it mean for the LGBT community to treat the church with "respect, compassion, and sensitivity"?

To answer this, it may be helpful to define these two communities. Of course, LGBT people are part of the church, so in a sense those questions imply a false dichotomy. The church is the entire "People of God," to use the language of the Second Vatican Council. So it is strange to discuss how the People of God can relate to a part of the People of God. In good Jesuit fashion, then, let me refine our terms.

When I refer to the church in this discussion I mean the *institutional church*—that is, the Vatican, the hierarchy, church leaders, the clergy, and all who work in an official capacity in the church.

Also, I will at times refer to both LGBT Catholics and the LGBT community. In fact, the church has relationships with both groups, because what it says about LGBT Catholics often reaches the ears of LGBT people who are not Catholic.

Let's begin by taking a walk on the first lane of the bridge, the one leading from the institutional church to the LGBT community, and reflect on what might it mean for the church to treat the LGBT community with "respect, compassion, and sensitivity."

Respect

First of all, *respect* means, at the very least, recognizing that the LGBT community *exists,* and extending to it the same recognition that any community desires and deserves because of its presence among us.

In the wake of the Orlando tragedy in 2016, when some church leaders spoke of the event without ever mentioning the words *LGBT* or *gay,* it revealed a certain failure to acknowledge the existence of this community. But this is not a Christian model, for Jesus recognizes all people, even those who seem invisible in the greater community. In fact, he reaches out specifically to those on the margins. Catholics, therefore, have a responsibility to make everyone feel visible and valuable.

Recognizing that LGBT Catholics exist has important pastoral implications. It means carrying out ministries to these communities, which some dioceses and parishes already do very well. Examples include celebrating Masses with LGBT groups, sponsoring diocesan and parish outreach programs, and in general helping LGBT Catholics feel that they are part of the church, that they are welcomed and loved.

Some Catholics have objected to this approach, saying that any outreach implies a tacit agreement with everything that anyone in the LGBT community says or does. This seems an unfair objection, because it is raised with virtually no other group. If a diocese sponsors, for example, an outreach group for Catholic business leaders, it does not mean that the diocese agrees with every value of corporate America. Nor does it mean that the church has sanctified everything that every businessman or businesswoman says or does. No one suggests that. Why not? Because people understand that the diocese is trying to help the members of that group feel more connected to their church, the church they belong to by virtue of their baptism.

Second, *respect* means calling a group what it asks to be called. On a personal level, if someone says to you, "I prefer to be called Jim instead of James," you would naturally listen and call him by the name he prefers. It's common courtesy.

It's the same on a group level. We don't use the term "Negroes" any longer. Why? Because that group feels more comfortable with other names, like "African Americans" or "blacks." Recently, I was told that "disabled persons" is not as acceptable as "people with disabilities." So now I'll use the latter term. Why? Because it is respectful to call people by the name they choose. Everyone has a right to the name they wish to be called by.

This is not a minor concern. In the Jewish and Christian traditions names are important.

In the Old Testament, God gives Adam and Eve the authority to name the creatures (Genesis 2:18–23). God also renames Abram as Abraham (17:4–6). A name in the Hebrew Scriptures stands for a person's identity; knowing a person's name meant, in a sense, that you knew the person. That is one reason why, when Moses asks to know God's name, God says, "I am who am" (Exodus 3:14–15)—in other words, as my Old Testament professor once explained to our class, "None of your business."

Later, in the New Testament, Jesus renames Simon as Peter (Matthew 16:18; John 1:42). The persecutor Saul renames himself Paul (Acts 13:9). Names are important in our church today as well. The first question a priest or deacon asks parents at an infant's baptism in the Catholic Church is, "What name do you give this child?"

Because names are important, church leaders are invited to be attentive to how they name the LGBT community. Let us lay to rest phrases like "afflicted with same-sex attraction," which no

LGBT person I know uses, and even "homosexual person," which seems overly clinical to many. Let's instead listen to what our gay brothers and lesbian sisters prefer to name themselves. Instead of prescribing what names to use, though "gay," "lesbian," "LGBT," and "LGBTQ" are the most common, I invite church leaders to recognize that people have a right to name themselves. Using those names is part of respect. And if Pope Francis and several of his cardinals and bishops can use the word *gay,* as they have done several times during his papacy, so can the rest of the church.

Respect also means acknowledging that LGBT Catholics bring unique gifts to the church— both as individuals and as a community. These gifts build up the church in special ways, as St. Paul wrote when he compared the People of God to a human body (1 Corinthians 12:12–27). Every body part is important: the hand, the eye, the foot. In fact, as Paul said, it is the parts of the body that "we think less honorable" that deserve even greater respect.

Many LGBT people have indeed felt "less honorable" in the church. So, following St. Paul, it is to these members and to their gifts that we should pay even *greater* respect. "Those members of the body that we think less honorable we clothe with greater honor," he writes.

Just consider for a moment the many gifts brought by LGBT Catholics who work in parishes, schools, chanceries, retreat centers, hospitals, and social service agencies. Let us "honor" them, as St. Paul says. As one example, some of the most gifted music ministers I have known in my almost thirty years as a Jesuit have been gay men who have brought tremendous joy to their parishes, week in and week out, during every liturgical season. They themselves are among the most joyful people I know in the church.

The church, as a whole, is invited to meditate on how LGBT Catholics build up the church with their presence, in the same way that elderly people, teenagers, women, people with disabilities, various ethnic groups, or any other groups build up a parish or a diocese. Although it is usually wrong to generalize, we can still pose the question: what might those gifts be?

Many, if not most, LGBT people have endured, from an early age, misunderstanding, prejudice, hatred, persecution, and even violence, and therefore often feel a natural compassion toward the marginalized. *Compassion* is a gift. They have often been made to feel unwelcome in their parishes and in their church, but they persevere because of their vigorous faith. *Perseverance* is a gift. They are often forgiving of clergy and other church employees who treat them like damaged goods. *Forgiveness* is a gift. Compassion, perseverance, and forgiveness are all gifts.

Let me add another gift: that of celibate priests and brothers who are gay, as well as chaste members of men's and women's religious orders who are gay or lesbian. Now, there are many reasons why almost no gay and lesbian clergy or members of religious orders are public about their sexuality. Among these reasons: they are simply private people; their bishops or religious superiors ask them not to speak about it; they themselves are uncomfortable with their sexuality; or they fear reprisals from parishioners.

But there are hundreds, perhaps thousands, of holy and hardworking gay clergy, and gay and lesbian members of religious orders, who live out their promises of celibacy and vows of chastity and help to build up the church. They freely give their whole selves to the church. They themselves are the gift.

Seeing, naming, and honoring all these gifts are components of respecting our LGBT brothers and sisters. So also is accepting them as beloved children of God and *letting them know* that they are beloved children of God. The church has a special call to proclaim God's love for a people who are often made to feel, whether by their families, neighbors, or religious leaders, as though they were damaged goods, unworthy of ministry, and even subhuman. The church is invited to both proclaim and demonstrate that LGBT people are beloved children of God.

Respect also should be extended to the work-place, especially if that workplace is a church or church-related organization. To that end, I'm saddened by the recent trend, in a few places, of the firing of LGBT men and women. Of course, church organizations have the authority to require their employees to follow church teachings. The problem is that this authority is applied in a highly *selective* way. Almost all the firings in recent years have focused on LGBT matters. Specifically, the firings have usually related to those employees who have entered into same-sex marriages, which is against church teaching, when one or the other partner has a public role in the church.

But if adherence to church teaching is going to be a litmus test for employment in Catholic institutions, then dioceses and parishes need to be consistent. Do we fire a straight man or woman who gets divorced and then remarries without an annulment? Divorce and remarriage of that sort are against church teaching. In fact, divorce is something Jesus himself forbade. Do we fire women who bear children out of wedlock? How about those living together without being married? Do we give pink slips to those who practice birth control? Those actions are against church teaching too.

And what about church employees who are not Catholic? If we fire employees who do not agree with or adhere to church teaching, do we fire all Protestants who work in a Catholic institution, because they do not believe in papal authority? That's an important church teaching. Do we fire Unitarians who do not believe in the Trinity?

Do we fire these people for such things? No, we do not. Why not? Because we are selective, perhaps unconsciously, perhaps consciously, about which church teachings matter.

Here is another way of looking at this kind of selectivity, one that shows us why it is problematic. Requiring church employees to adhere to church teachings means, at a more fundamental level, adhering to the Gospel. To be consistent, shouldn't we fire people for not helping the poor, for not being forgiving, or for not being loving?

That may sound odd, and it may even cause you to roll your eyes, but why should it? These commands of Jesus are the most essential "church teachings."

The selectivity of focus on LGBT matters when it comes to firings is, to use the words of the Catholic *Catechism,* a "sign of unjust discrimination" (No. 2358), something we are to avoid. Indeed, in 2016, *America* magazine published an editorial that said, "The high public profile of these firings, when combined with the apparent lack of due process and the absence of any comparable policing of marital status for heterosexual employees, constitute signs of 'unjust discrimination' and the church in the United States should do more to avoid them."

One young gay man once shared with me another perspective on this phenomenon. He wondered if the selectivity occurs not only because of homophobia, but because straight men and women are never forced to consider what would happen if they were gay. Thus it is easier for them to condemn homosexuality because they see themselves as now and forever straight. "You can never be a hypocrite preaching about the 'sinful homosexual lifestyle,'" he wrote in an e-mail, "because you will never find yourself where the temptation is present."

That was one reason he believed there was so much focus on this issue rather than other issues related to sexual morality—like divorce and pre-marital sex. Straight men and women might indeed engage in premarital sex or seek a divorce. But they are safe in condemning homosexuality because it will never be an experience they face. It is an interesting argument to consider.

Compassion

W hat would it mean for the institutional church to show compassion to LGBT men and women?

The word *compassion* (from the Greek *paschō*, "to suffer") means "to experience with, to suffer with." So what would it mean for the institutional church not only to respect LGBT Catholics, but to be with them, to experience life with them, and even to suffer with them?

This question can be asked not only about the hierarchy, but about the entire church. It can be asked not only about bishops and priests, but also about pastoral workers, directors of religious education, teachers, administrators, and those who don't work in any official capacity in the church but who participate in the life of the church as faithful parishioners: Catholic men and women of all sorts. How can all of us experience and suffer with our LGBT brothers and sisters?

The first and most essential requirement is listening. It is impossible to experience a person's life, or to be compassionate, if you do not listen to the person or if you do not ask questions.

Questions that Catholic leaders might ask their LGBT brothers and sisters are:

What was it like growing up as a gay boy, a lesbian girl, or a transgender person?

What is your life like now?

How have you suffered as a result of your orientation?

Where do you experience joy in your life?

What is your experience of God?

What is your experience of the church?

What do you hope for, long for, pray for?

They might also ask the parents of LGBT Catholics these kinds of questions:

What is it like for you to have an LGBT child?

What was it like when your child shared his or her sexuality with you?

Do you yourself feel welcome in the church?

Do you ever fear that your child will leave the church? And if your child has left, how are you dealing with that?

How might the church be a more welcoming place for your child?

What is your own experience of God?

What do you hope for, long for, pray for—
for both you and your child?

For the church to exercise compassion, we need to listen.

When we listen, we will hear the calls for help and prayer. And when our LGBT brothers and sisters are persecuted, church leaders are called to stand with them. In many parts of the world, LGBT persons are liable to experience appalling incidents of, in the words of the *Catechism,* "unjust discrimination"—prejudice, violence, and even murder. In some countries, a person can be jailed or executed for being gay or having same-sex relations.

In those countries, the institutional church has an absolute moral duty to stand up for its brothers and sisters, publicly. Sadly, this does not happen very often, and in fact a few church leaders have supported some of these discriminatory laws. But embedded in Catholic teaching is a call to stand with our LGBT brothers and sisters. The *Catechism* says "every sign of unjust discrimination" must be avoided. More fundamentally, helping someone, standing up for someone who is being beaten, is surely part of compassion. It is part of being a disciple of Jesus Christ. If you doubt that, read the Parable of the Good Samaritan (Luke 10:25–37).

Closer to home, what would it mean for the church in the United States to say, when needed, "It is wrong to treat the LGBT community like this"? Catholic leaders regularly publish statements—as they should—defending the unborn, refugees and migrants, the poor, the homeless, the aged.

This is one way to stand with people: by putting yourself out there, even taking heat for them.

But where are statements specifically in support of our LGBT brothers and sisters? When I ask this, some people say, "You can't compare what refugees face with what LGBT people face." As someone who worked with refugees in East Africa for two years, I know that's often the case. But it is important not to ignore the disproportionately high rates of suicide among LGBT youths and the fact that LGBT people are the victims of proportionally more hate crimes than any other minority group in this country. The bullying of LGBT students in schools is also an evil that should be squarely opposed, particularly given the Catholic Church's long history and extensive experience with running elementary, middle, and high schools.

As I've mentioned before, in the wake of the massacres at a gay nightclub in Orlando in 2016, when the LGBT community across the country was grieving, I was discouraged that more bishops did not immediately signal their support. Some did, of course. But imagine if the attacks were on, God forbid, a Methodist church. Many bishops would have said, "We stand with our Methodist brothers and sisters." Why didn't more Catholic leaders name our LGBT brothers and sisters in Orlando? To me, it seemed a failure of compassion, a failure to experience with, and a failure to suffer with. Orlando invites us all to reflect on this.

We need not look far for a model for this. God did this for all of us—in Jesus. The opening lines of the Gospel of John tell us, "The Word became flesh and lived among us" (1:14). The original Greek is more vivid: "The Word became flesh and pitched its tent among us" (*eskēnōsen en hēmin*). Isn't that a beautiful phrase? God entered our world to live among us. This is what Jesus did. He lived alongside us, took our side, even died like us.

This is what the church is called to do with all marginalized groups, as Pope Francis has often reminded us, including LGBT Catholics: to experience their lives and suffer with them.

And to be joyful with them as well! Because Jesus came to experience all parts of our lives, not just the sorrowful parts. LGBT people, though they may suffer persecution, share in the joys of the human condition. So, can you rejoice with our LGBT brothers and sisters?

Can the entire church—from the pope to the local bishops to priests to pastoral associates to parishioners—rejoice in the gifts and talents, the joy and enthusiasm brought by LGBT Catholics? Especially among younger LGBT people, I find a tremendous zest for the faith. Perhaps this is because, unlike their older brothers and sisters, they have grown up in a society where they feel more comfortable about their sexuality, and so they may feel less burdened by their sexual identity. (This is just my own supposition.) Overall, younger LGBT people who are active in the church bring a great many gifts, which we can celebrate and treasure.

We can celebrate and treasure more than simply their gifts. We can celebrate and treasure *them*. This is a kind of compassion too—to share in the experience of Christian joy that LGBT men and women, young and old, bring to the church.

Sensitivity

How can the institutional church be "sensitive" toward LGBT people? That's a beautiful word used by the *Catechism*.

Merriam-Webster's Dictionary defines *sensitivity* as "an awareness or understanding of the feelings of other people." That's related to Pope Francis's call for the church to be a church of "encounter" and "accompaniment."

To begin with, it is nearly impossible to know another person's feelings at a distance. You cannot understand the feelings of a community if you don't *know* the community. You can't be sensitive to the LGBT community if you only issue documents about them, preach about them, or tweet about them, without knowing them.

One reason the institutional church has struggled with sensitivity is that, based on my observations, many church leaders still do not know many gay and lesbian people. The temptation is to smile and say that church leaders *do* know people who are gay: priests and bishops who are not public about their homosexuality.

But my point is a larger one. Many church leaders do not know, on a personal level, LGBT people who are public about their sexuality. That lack of familiarity and friendship means it is more difficult to be sensitive. How can you be sensitive to people's situations if you don't know them? So, one invitation is for the hierarchy to come to know LGBT Catholics as friends.

In 2015 Cardinal Christoph Schönborn, the archbishop of Vienna, reminded us of this at the meeting of the Synod of Bishops on the Family, the gathering of Catholic bishops who assembled at the invitation of Pope Francis to discuss a wide variety of issues related to the family and, as it turned out, human sexuality.

Around that time, Cardinal Schönborn spoke of a gay couple he knew who had transformed his understanding of LGBT people. He even offered some qualified praise for his friend's same-sex union. The cardinal said:

> One shares one's life, one shares the joys and sufferings, one helps one another. We must recognize that this person has made an important step for his own good and for the good of others, even though, of course, this is not a situation that the church can consider regular.

He also overruled a priest in his archdiocese who had prohibited a man in a same-sex union from serving on a parish council. That is, Cardinal Schönborn stood with his LGBT brother. Much of this came from his experience of, knowledge of, and friendship with LGBT people.

Cardinal Schönborn said of the church, "It must accompany people."

In this, as in all things, Jesus is our model. When Jesus encountered people on the margins, he saw not categories but individuals. To be clear, I am not saying that the LGBT community should be, or should feel, marginalized. Rather, I am saying that within the church many of them do find themselves marginalized. They are seen as "other."

But for Jesus there was no "other."

Jesus saw beyond categories; he met people where they were and accompanied them. The Gospel of Matthew, for example, tells the story of Jesus meeting a Roman centurion who asked for healing for his servant (8:5–13). Although the man was not Jewish, Jesus saw a man in need and responded to his need.

In Luke's Gospel, Jesus meets Zacchaeus, the chief tax collector in Jericho (19:1–10). In that story, Zacchaeus, who is described as "short in stature," climbed a sycamore tree because "he wanted to see who Jesus was." When Jesus saw Zacchaeus perched in the tree, he saw a person seeking to encounter him. And even though he was the chief tax collector, and therefore would have been considered the "chief sinner" in that society, Jesus invited himself to Zacchaeus's house to meet with him over dinner.

Jesus was willing to be with, stand with, and befriend these people.

The movement for Jesus was always from the outside in. His message was always one of inclusion, communicated through speaking to people, healing them, and offering them what biblical scholars call "table fellowship," that is, dining with them, a sign of welcome and acceptance in first-century Palestine. In fact, Jesus was often criticized for this practice. But Jesus's movement was about inclusion. He was creating a sense of "us."

For with Jesus, there is no us and them. There is only us.

One common objection here is to say, "No, Jesus always told them, first of all, not to sin!" We cannot meet LGBT people because they are sinning, goes the argument, and when we do meet them, the first thing we must say is, "Stop sinning!"

But more often than not, this is not Jesus's way. In the story of the Roman centurion, Jesus doesn't shout "Pagan!" or scold him for not being Jewish. Instead, he professes amazement at the man's faith and then heals his servant. Likewise, in the story of Zacchaeus, after spying the tax collector perched in the tree, he doesn't point to him and shout, "Sinner!" Instead, Jesus says that he will dine at Zacchaeus's house, a public sign of openness and welcome, before Zacchaeus has said or done anything. Only *after* Jesus offers him welcome is Zacchaeus moved to conversion, promising to pay back anyone he might have defrauded.

For Jesus it is most often *community first*— meeting, encountering, including—*and conversion second.*

Pope Francis echoed this approach in an in-flight press conference in 2016, on his return to Rome from the countries of Georgia and Azerbaijan. "People must be accompanied, as Jesus accompanied," he said. "When a person who has this situation comes before Jesus, Jesus will surely not say: 'Go away because you're homosexual.'"

Sensitivity is based on encounter, accompaniment, and friendship.

Where does that lead? To the second meaning of *sensitivity,* which is, in common parlance, a heightened awareness of what might hurt or offend someone. When we are "sensitive" to people's situations, we are "sensitive" to anything that might needlessly offend.

One way to be sensitive is to consider the language we use. Some bishops have already called for the church to set aside the phrase "objectively disordered" when it comes to describing the homosexual inclination (as it is in the *Catechism,* No. 2358). The phrase relates to the orientation, not the person, but it is still needlessly hurtful. Saying that one of the deepest parts of a person—the part that gives and receives love—is "disordered" in itself is needlessly cruel.

Setting aside such language was discussed at the Synod on the Family, according to several news outlets. Later, in 2016, an Australian bishop, Vincent Long Van Nguyen, said in a lecture:

> We cannot talk about the integrity of creation, the universal and inclusive love of God, while at the same time colluding with the forces of oppression in the ill-treatment of racial minorities, women, and homosexual persons. . . . It won't wash with young people, especially when we purport to treat gay people with love and compassion and yet define their sexuality as "intrinsically disordered."

Part of sensitivity is understanding this.

Respect

Now let's take a walk on the other lane on the bridge, the one that leads from the LGBT community to the institutional church. What would it mean for LGBT Catholics to treat the institutional church with "respect, compassion, and sensitivity"?

In the church the hierarchy possesses institutional power. Members of the hierarchy have the power to allow individuals to receive the sacraments, to permit or prevent priests from celebrating the sacraments, to open or close diocesan or parish ministries, to allow people to retain their jobs in Catholic institutions, and so on.

But LGBT Catholics have power as well. Increasingly, for instance, the Western media has been more sympathetic to the LGBT community than to the Catholic hierarchy. That's a kind of power.

Still, in the institutional church, it is the hierarchy that operates from the position of power.

LGBT Catholics are called to treat those in power with "respect, compassion, and sensitivity." Why? Because, as I mentioned, it's a two-way bridge. More important, LGBT Catholics are Christians, and those virtues express Christian love. Those virtues also help to build up the entire community.

For many LGBT Catholics this may be a challenge or even painful to hear, given how they have been treated. I only invite them to meditate on what the words "respect, compassion, and sensitivity" mean when applied to their relationship with the church. This is the moment to set aside the us-and-them mentality, for there is no us and them in the church.

What would it mean for the LGBT community to show "respect" to the church? Here again, I am speaking specifically about the pope and the bishops—that is, the hierarchy and, more broadly, the *magisterium,* the teaching authority of the church.

Catholics believe that bishops, priests, and deacons receive at their ordinations the grace for a special ministry of leadership in the church. We also believe that bishops have an authority that comes down to them from the apostles. That is what we mean, in part, when we profess our belief each Sunday at Mass that the church is "apostolic." Also, we believe that the Holy Spirit inspires and guides the church. Certainly that happens through the People of God, who, as the Second Vatican Council says, are imbued with the Spirit, but it also happens through popes, bishops, and clergy by virtue of their ordination and their offices.

The institutional church—popes and councils, archbishops and bishops—speak with authority in their role as teachers. They don't all speak with the same level of authority (more about that later), but Catholics must prayerfully consider what they are teaching. To do that, we are called to listen. Their teaching deserves our respect.

So, first, we are called to listen. On all matters, not just LGBT issues, the episcopacy speaks with authority and draws from a great well of tradition. When bishops speak on matters like, but not confined to, love, forgiveness, and mercy; as well as caring for the poor, the marginalized, the unborn, the homeless, prisoners, refugees, and so on, they are drawing not only from the Gospels, but from the spiritual treasury of the church's tradition. Often, especially on social justice issues, they will challenge us with a wisdom that we will hear nowhere else in the world.

When they speak about LGBT matters in a way that LGBT Catholics don't agree with or that angers or even offends them, LGBT Catholics are invited to challenge themselves to listen more closely. Ask: "What are they saying? Why are they saying it? What lies behind their words?"

LGBT Catholics are called to listen, consider, pray, and of course use their informed consciences as they discern how to live their lives.

Beyond what one might call ecclesial respect, the hierarchy deserves simple human respect. Often I'm saddened by the things that I hear some LGBT Catholics and their allies saying about certain bishops. I hear these things privately, but also publicly. Recently one LGBT group, in response to a statement from bishops on same-sex marriage, said that the bishops should stop being "locked in their ivory towers." I thought, "Really? You're saying that to bishops in poor dioceses too? That they live in 'ivory towers'? To bishops who minister to the poor, oversee parishes in inner-city neighborhoods, sponsor schools that educate the inner-city poor, and manage Catholic Charities offices?" You may disagree with the bishops, but that kind of language is not only disrespectful; it's inaccurate.

More seriously, LGBT Catholics and their allies sometimes mock bishops for their promises of celibacy, their residences, and especially the clothes they wear. The barely disguised implication of posting online photos of bishops wearing elaborate liturgical vestments is that they are effeminate, they are hypocrites, or they are repressed gay men.

Does the LGBT community want to proceed in that way? Do gay men want to mock bishops as effeminate, when many gay men were most likely teased about precisely that when they were young? Is that not simply perpetuating hatred? How can people castigate a bishop for not respecting the LGBT community when they themselves do not afford him respect in the process? Is it right for people to critique others for their supposed un-Christian attitudes by themselves being un-Christian?

Some people think that this is a justifiable condemnation of what they see as hypocrisy. One gay man told me that he felt that it was not only justifiable but "therapeutic," particularly when it was directed against church leaders who had, in his words, "said some awful stuff about gays."

But I invite LGBT people to think about this question. Is this in keeping with our Christian call? To me, it seems a perpetuation of a cycle of hatred.

This may be very hard for people who feel beaten down by the church to hear. One gay friend recently told me that this mockery comes not from a place of hatred, but from a sense of betrayal. "Knowing that there are some gay members in the hierarchy," he wrote to me recently, "it is both frustrating and heartbreaking to hear them preach down to LGBT laypeople."

But being respectful of people with whom you disagree is at the heart of the Christian way. And part of this is surely about forgiveness, an essential Christian virtue.

Even from a human point of view, it's good strategy. If you sincerely want to influence the church's perspective on LGBT matters, it helps to earn the trust of the members of the hierarchy. One way to do that is by respecting them.

So both the Christian approach and simple human wisdom would say: "Respect them."

Compassion

What would it mean to show compassion to the hierarchy?

First, let's recall the definition of *compassion:* "to experience with or suffer with." Part of this, as I mentioned, is knowing what a person's life is like. Part of compassion toward the institutional church, then, is a real understanding of the life of those in power.

In my life as a Jesuit, I have met many cardinals, archbishops, and bishops. Quite a few I consider friends. All the ones I've met are kind, hardworking, and prayerful men, many of whom have been very kind to me personally, loyal servants of the church trying to carry out the ministries for which they were ordained.

These days, in addition to the normal "triple ministry" of bishops to "teach, govern, and sanctify" (that is, teach the Gospel, run the diocese, and celebrate the sacraments), bishops have to do the following:

Staff parishes in the face of rapidly declining vocations to the priesthood and religious orders;

Deal with the fallout—financial, legal, and emotional—from clergy sex-abuse cases, usually cases they had nothing to do with;

Decide which parishes and schools to close or consolidate in the face of emotional pleas and angry protests from parishioners, neighbors, students, and alumni;

Help raise money for nearly every institution in their diocese, including schools, hospitals, retirement communities for priests, and social service agencies;

In some cases deal with a growing diocese and increased numbers of parishioners in the face of a lack of resources and infrastructure; and

Answer complaints from furious Catholics that pour into their chanceries about everything you can imagine, including supposed liturgical abuses during Mass, stray comments a priest made in a homily, an article they didn't like in the diocesan newspaper, even the fact that a Catholic received an award from a group they don't like.

Not seeing these church leaders in the context of their complicated duties is not only to miss the truth of the situation; it signals a lack of compassion, which hampers receptivity of the message being communicated.

Compassion also leads us to what might be called an "equality of heart." That means coming to see that at least a few in positions of leadership in the church may themselves be struggling. They might be homosexual men who at a younger age were tortured by the same hateful attitudes that most LGBT people experienced growing up and who entered a religious world that seemed to afford them some safety and privacy.

The Irish novelist Colm Toíbín, writing in the *London Review of Books* in 2010, offered a perceptive and sympathetic summary of what this might have been like. He recalled attending a workshop, at age sixteen, for boys who believed they had a vocation to the priesthood:

Some of the reasons why gay men became priests are obvious and simple; others are not. Becoming a priest, first of all, seemed to solve the problem of not wanting others to know that you were queer. As a priest, you could be celibate or unmarried, and everyone would understand the reasons. It was because you had a vocation; you had been called by God, had been specially chosen by him. For other boys, the idea of never having sex with a woman was something they could not even entertain. For you, such sex was problematic; thus you had no blueprint for an easy future. The prospect, on the other hand, of making a vow in holiness never to have sex with a woman offered you relief. The idea that you might want to have sex with men, that you might be "that way inclined," as they used to say, was not even mentioned, not once, during that workshop in which everything under the sun was discussed.

These are far from the only reasons that some gay men enter diocesan seminaries and religious houses of formation. In general, gay priests and members of religious orders enter for the same reasons that their straight counterparts do: they feel called by God to follow the Gospel in this way, to serve the church in this way, to help people in this way. Still, those other reasons may have been additional factors in the appeal of that life: a certain privacy, a way to serve God without having to admit one's sexuality. A few may have remained with that worldview, even as, over the last few decades, the truth about being gay gradually became more easily understood and less terrifying to live with.

This is what it is like to have been burdened by the effects of the hatred of gays and lesbians, particularly the deep-seated hatred that existed decades ago, and not being able to admit a deep part of oneself. So LGBT Catholics are invited to feel for and pray for these our brothers, even when their own backgrounds sometimes have led them to behave as if they were the enemies of the LGBT community.

The invitation here is to see these bishops in their humanity, in their complexity, and amid the burdens of their ministries. I know this may be difficult for some LGBT people, but there is Christian compassion in trying to do this.

Many LGBT people feel that the institutional church or a few priests and bishops have persecuted them. They see these men as their enemies or, at the very least, as men who misunderstand them. And sadly, some bishops, priests, and deacons have indeed said and done ignorant, hurtful, and even hateful things.

One gay friend of mine said that he was particularly angry in the wake of the clergy sex-abuse crisis. After years of trying to stay with the church, despite feeling unwelcome, he felt deeply betrayed by the institution. "I was furious," he told me. How could he accept condemnations of his own sexuality from members of the hierarchy who had covered up the crime of sex abuse?

Over the years in my counseling of LGBT men and women I have heard many depressing stories of stray comments made by priests in homilies or in private conversations that betray the most hateful attitudes toward LGBT people. Over and over, I would hear the same question: "How can I stay in a church that treats me like this?"

But I believe that these actions represent a minority in the hierarchy and in the clergy, albeit one that until recently seemed to hold some sway in the church; that the tide is slowly changing; and that Pope Francis's papacy and the actions of many church leaders today are helping to heal some of that hurt. Many church leaders—bishops and priests—manifest a deep understanding of the hurt that LGBT Catholics have felt.

In the wake of the shootings at the Pulse nightclub in Orlando, for example, Bishop Robert Lynch, of St. Petersburg, Florida, who has since retired, wrote this on his blog:

> Sadly it is religion, including our own, which targets, mostly verbally, and also often breeds contempt for gays, lesbians and transgender people. Attacks today on LGBT men and women often plant the seed of contempt, then hatred, which can ultimately lead to violence. Those women

and men who were mowed down early yesterday morning were all made in the image and likeness of God. We teach that. We should believe that. We must stand for that. Without yet knowing who perpetrated the Pulse mass murders, when I saw the Imam come forward at a press conference yesterday morning, I knew that somewhere in the story there would be a search to find religious roots. While deranged people do senseless things, all of us observe, judge and act from some kind of religious background. Singling out people for victimization because of their religion, their sexual orientation, their nationality must be offensive to God's ears. It has to stop also.

Many Catholic leaders do stand with the LGBT community.

Still, what is the Christian response if some LGBT Catholics feel continuing hostility toward select Catholic leaders?

By way of a suggestion, let me tell you a story.

When I was twenty-seven, I told my parents I was entering the Jesuits. I sprang the news on them with absolutely no warning; I hadn't even told them I was considering it. Not surprisingly, they were confused and upset. They saw the decision as reckless. And that confused and upset me.

I wondered, "How could they not see what I was doing? How could they not understand me?" In response, my spiritual director said, "You've had twenty-seven years to get used to this, Jim. And you just sprang it on them. Give them the gift of time."

Challenging as it may be to hear, and without setting aside the great suffering that LGBT people have experienced in the church, I wonder if the LGBT community could give the institutional church the gift of time—time to get to know each other. In a very real way, an open and public LGBT community is a new thing, even in my lifetime. In a very real way, the world is just getting to know that community. So is the church. I know it's a burden, but it's perhaps not surprising. It takes time to get to know people. So perhaps the LGBT community can give the institutional church the gift of patience.

If, even after all this, some still perceive a few church leaders as enemies, the deeper Christian response is to pray for them. And that's not me talking: that's the Jesus of the Gospels.

What do I mean by praying for them? Not simply the condescending prayer that says, "God, help them not to be such terrible people," but a sincere prayer for their well-being. Of course, we can pray for a person's conversion, particularly someone who seems unwilling to show mercy and compassion toward others, but prayer should always be done with a loving heart. True prayer wants others to flourish.

If any still have a hard time praying for church leaders, they might use a prayer that I find helpful when I am struggling with another person. My prayer is to see that person as God sees him or her.

This prayer, in my experience, is always answered.

Sensitivity

Let's return to the beautiful word *sensitivity*. Again, we can use it to mean not denigrating the bishops or the hierarchy. And again, that is not only simple human courtesy; it is Christian charity.

But I would like to use *sensitivity* in another way. I would like to invite the LGBT community to more deeply consider who is speaking and how they are speaking. Here I'm turning to theology—specifically ecclesiology, the branch of Christian theology that looks at the church itself. I would like to focus on the theological idea—which is part of Catholic teaching—of different "levels of authority."

As Catholics, we believe in various levels of teaching authority in our church. Not every church official speaks with the same level of authority.

The simplest way of explaining this is that what your local pastor says in a homily does not come from the same level of authority as what the pope says in an encyclical. The different levels of authoritative teaching begin with the Gospels, which are followed by the documents of church councils and then papal pronouncements. Even the different papal pronouncements have various levels of authority. Among those with the highest authority are constitutions or encyclicals, addressed to the whole church; followed by apostolic letters and *motu proprios;* then the pope's daily homilies, speeches, and press conferences, and so on. There are also documents from synods and individual Vatican congregations and, on the local level, documents from bishops' conferences and pastoral letters from local bishops.

Each has a different level of authority. They all need to be prayerfully read, but it is important to know that they do not all have equal authority.

Of course, the hierarchy is not the only group that speaks with authority. Authority resides in holiness as well. Holy men and women who are not members of the hierarchy, like St. Teresa of Calcutta, and holy laypeople, like Dorothy Day or Jean Vanier, speak with authority.

Also, it's important to be careful about taking what the mainstream media says about "church teaching" at face value. Recently I read a headline that said, "Keep Homilies to Eight Minutes, Vatican Tells Clergy." I thought, "The Vatican says this?" Sure enough, when I read the article, I discovered that it came from an individual bishop working in the Vatican who was offering his own suggestions to preachers. The headline was false. The "Vatican" wasn't doing any such thing. So, again, sensitivity is in order.

Moreover, we need to be "sensitive" to the fact that when Vatican officials speak—whether the pope or a Vatican congregation—they are speaking to the entire world, not just the West and certainly not just the United States. A topic that seems tepid in the United States might be shocking in Latin America or Africa.

To that end, I was disappointed in the reaction of some LGBT Catholics in this country to the pope's apostolic exhortation on family life, *Amoris Laetitia,* "The Joy of Love."

In that document, Pope Francis says:

> We would like before all else to reaffirm that every person, regardless of sexual orientation, ought to be respected in his or her dignity and treated with consideration, while "every sign of unjust discrimination" is to be carefully avoided, particularly any form of aggression and violence. Such families should be given respectful pastoral guidance, so that those who manifest a homosexual orientation can receive the assistance they need to understand and fully carry out God's will in their lives. (No. 250)

"*Before all else,*" the pope says, LGBT people should be treated with dignity. That's an immense statement, and, by the way, nowhere does he mention anything about an "objective disorder." Nonetheless, among some LGBT people in this country those lines were dismissed with cries of "Not enough!"

Perhaps in the West those words seemed insufficient. But the pope is writing not simply for the West, much less simply for the United States. Imagine reading that in a country where violence against LGBT people is rampant or even the norm, and the church has remained silent. What is bland in the United States is incendiary in other parts of the world. What might be obvious to a bishop in one country is a clear, forceful, or even threatening challenge to a bishop in another country. What seems arid to LGBT people in one country may be, to those in another country, water in a barren desert.

By the same token, there is a role for prophecy. Prophets are sometimes called to say things that make others uncomfortable, even angry, out of their love for God and others. The prophet both points people ahead to the future that God holds out to them and calls people back to the source of their love: God. Yet prophetic speech does not have to devolve into yelling and shaming.

Doubtless many readers will think of Jesus turning over the tables of the money changers in the Temple or excoriating religious leaders of his day: "But woe to you, scribes and Pharisees, hypocrites! For you lock people out of the kingdom of heaven" (Matthew 23:13). Or John the Baptist, standing in his camel-hair garment by the Jordan River, doing the same: "When he saw many Pharisees and Sadducees coming for baptism, he said to them, 'You brood of vipers! Who warned you to flee from the wrath to come?'" (Matthew 3:7) There is a place for this kind of prophecy, and it has been exercised by some of the greatest saints in the Christian tradition. But it must be exercised with great care. For none of us are John the Baptist, the ascetical prophet, much less Jesus, the sinless one.

I'm not saying that one should never be angry. Anger is a natural human emotion and a legitimate response to injustice. Jesus himself was angered when he saw injustice. But those who feel called to that distinctive kind of prophetic ministry should always do it from a place of love. They are called to ask themselves: "Is this true prophecy? Where does the desire to be prophetic come from? How is God in this? Am I doing this out of love?"

Overall, all of us need to discern carefully. So we are called to be sensitive in many ways.

Together on the Bridge

You've been invited to walk on a bridge built from the three pillars of the *Catechism*'s approach to LGBT ministry: "respect, compassion, and sensitivity."

Some of this may be hard for members of the LGBT community to hear. Some of this also may be challenging for bishops and Catholic leaders to hear. This is because neither lane on that bridge is smooth. On this bridge, as in life, there are tolls. It costs when you live a life of respect, compassion, and sensitivity. But to trust in that bridge is to trust that eventually people will be able to cross back and forth easily, and that the hierarchy and the LGBT community will be able to encounter one another, accompany one another, and love one another.

It is also to trust that God desires forgiveness. It is to trust that God desires reconciliation. It is to trust that God desires unity.

We are all on the bridge together. For that bridge is the church. And, ultimately, on the other side of the bridge for each group is welcome, community, and love.

In conclusion, I would like to say something specifically to the Catholic LGBT community. In difficult times you might ask: "What keeps the bridge standing? What keeps it from collapsing onto the sharp rocks? What keeps us from plunging into the dangerous waters below?"

The answer is: the Holy Spirit.

The Holy Spirit, which is supporting the church, is supporting *you,* for you are beloved children of God who, by virtue of your baptism, have as much right to be in the church as the pope, your local bishop, and me.

Of course, that bridge has some loose stones, big bumps, and deep potholes, because the people in our church are not perfect. We never have been—just ask St. Peter. And we never will be. We are all imperfect people, struggling to do our best in the light of our individual vocations. We are all pilgrims on the way, loved sinners following the call we first heard at our baptism and that we continue to hear every day of our lives.

In short, you are not alone. Millions of your Catholic brothers and sisters accompany you, as do your bishops, as we journey imperfectly together on this bridge.

More important, we are accompanied by God, the reconciler of all men and women as well as the architect, the builder, and the foundation of that bridge.

Biblical
Passages for
Reflection
and
Meditation

Sometimes when discussing controversial topics with those with whom we disagree, it is easy to lose track of what we hold in common. All Christians have access to the spiritual riches found in the Scriptures, which, after all, were written amid the spiritual turmoil and social conflicts of the writers' times. We can learn from those who went before us. That is one reason why active reflection and meditation on Scripture can be such a rich and illuminating spiritual practice.

As spiritual resources for those in the LGBT community, below I have collected biblical passages and provided accompanying questions that can serve as aids to either personal or communal reflection. The first group includes biblical passages referred to in the essay "A Two-Way Bridge." Later come passages that I have found, through my ministry, to consistently speak to LBGT people and their families and friends.

All of these beautiful passages are not just for LGBT people, but can be used by everyone, especially those who hope to welcome them into community.

You can use these passages any way you wish, but let me offer a few suggestions.

First, after each passage or group of passages on the same topic, I offer reflection questions to help you meditate more deeply about what these passages might say to you. Remember that God speaks powerfully through the Bible, the living word of God. You might think about these questions, and then imagine yourself in God's presence (which you always are, but you are perhaps more conscious of it when you pray) and share your answers with God. Some find "journaling," writing down what happens in your prayer, helpful. Some even find writing a letter to God helpful.

Second, one of the spiritual traditions of my religious order is a technique popularized by St. Ignatius Loyola, the founder of the Jesuits, in which you imagine yourself in a Scripture scene with as much vividness as possible. You ask yourself: "What do I see? What do I hear? What do I feel? What do I smell? What do I taste?" With God's help, you try to "place" yourself in the Bible scene imaginatively.

This method of prayer may strike you as odd, but since your imagination is part of God's gift to you, God can work through it. Often this technique can help you see the passage in a new way. You might, for example, be reading about Jesus healing a sick person, recognize the need for healing in your own life, and be moved to ask God for help in that area.

For some passages this technique may not work as well—St. Paul's letters, for example, are in general not stories but didactic missives. They may lend themselves more to a kind of quiet meditation, where the primary fruit of prayer is a new insight or a deeper understanding.

But in the Old and New Testaments, many passages lend themselves easily to the imaginative kind of "Ignatian" prayer. In the stories of Jesus encountering people with a variety of hopes and desires, try to imagine yourself in the scene, and see what sort of feelings, memories, insights, desires, and emotions arise in you. Then pay attention to them and share what happens in prayer with God.

Third, you might allow God to speak to you in a quieter way. That is, you might simply sit silently with a passage, or even a single word, without needing to imagine yourself in any "scene." The prayer here is less concerned with images and is more free-form. Then you might discover that the passage evokes a feeling of calm or comfort, or a desire to act or advocate. See in those feelings and desires God's reaching out to you.

In the end, there is no "right" way to pray. Whatever way you use these passages is up to you.

Finally, the reflection questions can be used in group settings either as discussion topics or aids to communal prayer. I've included questions for both LGBT people as well as their families, friends, and allies.

On Names and
Naming

Names are important in the Old and New Testaments. Names often communicate something essential about a person. "Isaac," for example, the name of the son of Abraham and Sarah, means "He laughs" or "laughter," since Sarah had laughed when she heard that she would bear a son in her old age (Genesis 18:12). The name "Jesus" (Yeshua) means "The Lord saves." To know another person's name was to have a certain level of knowledge of, and even intimacy with, the person.

God allows Adam ("the man") to name the creatures:

> Out of the ground the LORD God formed every animal of the field and every bird of the air, and brought them to the man to see what he would call them; and whatever the man called every living creature, that was its name. The man gave names to all cattle, and to the birds of the air, and to every animal of the field. (Genesis 2:19–20)

God renames Abram:

> No longer shall your name be Abram, but your name shall be Abraham; for I have made you the ancestor of a multitude of nations. (Genesis 17:5)

Moses asks to know God's name:

> Then the LORD said [to Moses], "I have observed the misery of my people who are in Egypt; I have heard their cry on account of their taskmasters. So come,

I will send you to Pharaoh to bring my people, the Israelites, out of Egypt."

But Moses said to God, "If I come to the Israelites and say to them, 'The God of your ancestors has sent me to you,' and they ask me, 'What is his name?' what shall I say to them?" God said to Moses, "I AM WHO I AM." He said further, "Thus you shall say to the Israelites, 'I AM has sent me to you.'" God also said to Moses, "Thus you shall say to the Israelites, 'The LORD, the God of your ancestors, the God of Abraham, the God of Isaac, and the God of Jacob, has sent me to you.'" (Exodus 3:7, 10, 13–15)

Reflection Questions

1. By what name do you call God? *Lord? Creator? Friend?* What is God's name for you?

2. Can you name a few of the people who have been the most helpful in your spiritual journey? Name them in God's presence and offer thanks for their help.

3. When you think of your own sexual orientation, what word do you use? Why? Can you speak to God about this in prayer?

4. Try imagining yourself in Moses's place. What would it be like to talk to God directly? How do you think you might feel while God spoke? What would you have said or asked?

5. *For families, friends, and allies:* How did you feel when you first heard of your family member or friend name his or her sexuality? Did that "naming" change or deepen your relationship with that person? What does that say to you about your own relationship with God?

Different Gifts

In the First Letter to the Corinthians, St. Paul presents an image of the church as a body whose members all contribute to its functioning. All of us bring different gifts to the church, no matter who we are. Some of us might have a talent for organizing and can help arrange events. Others might have a talent for music and serve in liturgical settings. Others of us love theology and use it to help explain our faith to others. All of us make up the "Body of Christ," a traditional image of the church. Notice too how St. Paul focuses on the parts of the body that are "less honorable." Sometimes LGBT people are, tragically, made to feel that way, but, as Paul says, it is precisely these people who deserve even greater respect.

> For just as the body is one and has many members, and all the members of the body, though many, are one body, so it is with Christ. For in the one Spirit we were all baptized into one body—Jews or Greeks, slaves or free—and we were all made to drink of one Spirit.
>
> Indeed, the body does not consist of one member but of many. If the foot would say, "Because I am not a hand, I do not belong to the body," that would not make it any less a part of the body. And if the ear would say, "Because I am not an eye, I do not belong to the body," that would not make it any less a part of the body. If the whole body were

an eye, where would the hearing be?
If the whole body were hearing, where
would the sense of smell be? But as it
is, God arranged the members in the
body, each one of them, as he chose. If
all were a single member, where would
the body be? As it is, there are many
members, yet one body. The eye cannot
say to the hand, "I have no need of
you," nor again the head to the feet, "I
have no need of you." On the contrary,
the members of the body that seem to
be weaker are indispensable, and those
members of the body that we think less
honorable we clothe with greater honor,
and our less respectable members are
treated with greater respect; whereas our
more respectable members do not need
this. But God has so arranged the body,
giving the greater honor to the inferior
member, that there may be no dissension
within the body, but the members may

have the same care for one another. If one member suffers, all suffer together with it; if one member is honored, all rejoice together with it.

Now you are the body of Christ and individually members of it.
(1 Corinthians 12:12–27)

Reflection Questions

1. What gifts do you bring to the church? Can you thank God for these gifts?

2. How have you exercised those gifts?

3. Has anyone ever prevented you from exercising your gifts? Can you express how you feel about that to God?

4. St. Paul says that the "members" of the body (or church) who have been the least respected should be honored the most. Does that make sense to you?

5. What gifts from others in the church have helped you move closer to God? That is, who has helped you on your journey?

6. *For families, friends, and allies:* Have LGBT people brought their gifts to your own life and your own ministry? How do you recognize those gifts? Has your ministry lost out on gifts because of prejudices? What might you do to ameliorate those prejudices?

Care for Those
Who Are
Persecuted

Most people know Jesus's Parable of the Good Samaritan, but after spending time reflecting on it, many are still surprised by it. A parable is not meant to have only one meaning. The biblical scholar C. H. Dodd wrote, in a well-known definition, that a parable "teases the mind into active thought." Parables are stories designed to open one's mind and heart to the mystery of God.

For me, this famous parable shows us not only the need to care for those who are persecuted, but also how help can come from someone completely unexpected. The Samaritans were considered the enemies of the Jewish people. And so there is a turnaround here. The person we hate turns out to be the person we need.

> Just then a lawyer stood up to test Jesus. "Teacher," he said, "what must I do to inherit eternal life?" He said to him, "What is written in the law? What do you read there?" He answered, "You shall love the Lord your God with all your heart, and with all your soul, and with all your strength, and with all your mind; and your neighbor as yourself." And he said to him, "You have given the right answer; do this, and you will live."

But wanting to justify himself, he asked Jesus, "And who is my neighbor?" Jesus replied, "A man was going down from Jerusalem to Jericho, and fell into the hands of robbers, who stripped him, beat him, and went away, leaving him half dead. Now by chance a priest was going down that road; and when he saw him, he passed by on the other side. So likewise a Levite, when he came to the place and saw him, passed by on the other side. But a Samaritan while traveling came near him; and when he saw him, he was moved with pity. He went to him and bandaged his wounds, having poured oil and wine on them. Then he put him on his own animal, brought him to an inn, and took care of him. The next day he took out two denarii, gave them to the innkeeper, and said, 'Take care of him; and when I come back, I will repay you whatever more you spend.' Which of these three, do you think, was a neighbor to the man who fell into the hands of the robbers?" He said, "The one who showed him mercy." Jesus said to him, "Go and do likewise." (Luke 10:25–37)

Reflection Questions

1. When have you been a "Good Samaritan"?

2. When has someone unexpected or surprising cared for you?

3. Has anyone you hated ever unexpectedly helped you?

4. Think of individuals you dislike, perhaps in the church. Can you pray to be a "Good Samaritan" to them? Can you pray that one day you might be open to receiving help from them in some way?

5. How has God "bandaged" your wounds?

6. *For families, friends, and allies:* How have LGBT people been "Good Samaritans" to you? How are you called to be a "Good Samaritan" in return? Have you ever experienced any surprises in your relationships with your LGBT friends or family members? What does that say to you about God?

Jesus Meets People
Where They Are

In the story of Jesus's healing of the Roman centurion's servant, notice that Jesus does not castigate the Roman centurion for not being Jewish. Jesus accepts the centurion as he is and does what the man asks: he heals his servant.

> When [Jesus] entered Capernaum, a centurion came to him, appealing to him and saying, "Lord, my servant is lying

at home paralyzed, in terrible distress."
And he said to him, "I will come and
cure him." The centurion answered,
"Lord, I am not worthy to have you
come under my roof; but only speak the
word, and my servant will be healed.
For I also am a man under authority,
with soldiers under me; and I say to
one, 'Go,' and he goes, and to another,
'Come,' and he comes, and to my slave,
'Do this,' and the slave does it." When
Jesus heard him, he was amazed and
said to those who followed him, "Truly
I tell you, in no one in Israel have I
found such faith. I tell you, many will
come from east and west and will eat
with Abraham and Isaac and Jacob in
the kingdom of heaven, while the heirs
of the kingdom will be thrown into
the outer darkness, where there will be
weeping and gnashing of teeth." And to
the centurion Jesus said, "Go; let it be
done for you according to your faith."

And the servant was healed in that hour.
(Matthew 8:5–13)

Reflection Questions

1. Does it surprise you that Jesus helped someone who was a "pagan"?

2. What does Jesus's welcome of the centurion say to you about God's welcome?

3. When you imagine this story, what do you think the Roman centurion's response was like? Have you ever experienced a surprising welcome?

4. What does the centurion's faith say to you? How can it influence your own?

5. *For families, friends, and allies:* Your family member or friend has confided in you and relied on you. Have you ever been amazed, as Jesus was, by the trust that has

been placed in you? How does that make you feel toward the one who trusts you? Toward God?

✦ ✦

Likewise, when Jesus meets Zacchaeus, Jesus does not castigate the "chief sinner" in the area. Rather, he encounters him and offers him "table fellowship," which leads to the man's change of heart. Notice that for Jesus it is most often community first, conversion second. Also notice that Zacchaeus, like so many of us, wants to see "who Jesus was." When the crowd prevents him from doing so, he takes matters into his own hands. It's a reminder not to let others who might "grumble" against us get in the way of our encountering Jesus.

> [Jesus] entered Jericho and was passing through it. A man was there named Zacchaeus; he was a chief tax collector

and was rich. He was trying to see who Jesus was, but on account of the crowd he could not, because he was short in stature. So he ran ahead and climbed a sycamore tree to see him, because he was going to pass that way. When Jesus came to the place, he looked up and said to him, "Zacchaeus, hurry and come down; for I must stay at your house today." So he hurried down and was happy to welcome him. All who saw it began to grumble and said, "He has gone to be the guest of one who is a sinner." Zacchaeus stood there and said to the Lord, "Look, half of my possessions, Lord, I will give to the poor; and if I have defrauded anyone of anything, I will pay back four times as much." Then Jesus said to him, "Today salvation has come to this house, because he too is a son of Abraham. For the Son of Man came to seek out and to save the lost." (Luke 19:1–10)

Reflection Questions

1. Zacchaeus wanted to see "who Jesus was." Who is Jesus for you?

2. The tax collector could not see "on account of the crowd." When have others, or the opinions of others, prevented you from moving closer to God?

3. The insight about "community first, conversion second" comes from the biblical scholar Ben Meyer. He contrasts Jesus's approach to that of John the Baptist, who asked for repentance first. Of course, we all need to repent, and are all called to continual conversion, but what does Jesus's approach say to you about the church? And about you?

4. *For families, friends, and allies:* The crowd "grumbles" when Jesus offers Zacchaeus

welcome. That is, they seem to oppose Jesus's outreach. When have you stood up for your LGBT family member or friend? Have you ever thought of your support as the work of Jesus? Perhaps you might share this experience with Jesus in prayer.

You Are "Wonderfully Made"

In Psalm 139, the psalmist tells us that God created us, knows us intimately, and understands us. The image of God "knitting" us together in our mothers' wombs is a vivid reminder that we are "wonderfully made" by the God who created us. Of all the passages in the Bible, this one, in my experience, has proven to

be the most helpful for LGBT people and their
family and friends.

O LORD, you have searched me and
kn-own me.
You know when I sit down and when I
rise up;
you discern my thoughts from far
away.
You search out my path and my lying
down,
and are acquainted with all my
ways.
Even before a word is on my tongue,
O LORD, you know it completely.
You hem me in, behind and before,
and lay your hand upon me.
Such knowledge is too wonderful
for me;
it is so high that I cannot attain it.

Where can I go from your spirit?
Or where can I flee from your
presence?
If I ascend to heaven, you are there;
if I make my bed in Sheol, you
are there.
If I take the wings of the morning
and settle at the farthest limits of
the sea,
even there your hand shall lead me,
and your right hand shall hold me
fast.
If I say, "Surely the darkness shall
cover me,
and the light around me become
night,"
even the darkness is not dark to you;
the night is as bright as the day,
for darkness is as light to you.

For it was you who formed my inward
parts;
you knit me together in my
mother's womb.
I praise you, for I am fearfully and
wonderfully made.
Wonderful are your works;
that I know very well.
My frame was not hidden
from you,
when I was being made in secret,
intricately woven in the depths of
the earth.
Your eyes beheld my unformed
substance.
In your book were written
all the days that were formed
for me,
when none of them as yet existed.
How weighty to me are your thoughts,
O God!
How vast is the sum of them!

I try to count them—they are more than
the sand;

I come to the end—I am still with
you. (Psalm 139:1–18)

Reflection Questions

1. Think about what it means for you to be
"wonderfully made." Can you praise God,
as the psalmist does? What would your
praise look like?

2. What is it like to think of God forming
you in your "mother's womb"?

3. The psalmist admits that God's ways are
beyond the human capacity to understand,
and yet the psalmist is "still with" God.
What do you think gives the psalmist that
kind of faith?

4. God, who creates only good things, made
your "inward parts." How does that make

you feel about yourself? Can you tell God in your own words how you feel?

5. St. Augustine said, "God is nearer to me than I am to myself" (*interior intimo meo*). What is it like to imagine God knowing you so intimately, as the psalmist does?

6. *For families, friends, and allies:* You are wonderfully made yourself! And your family member or friend is made in a different, but no less wonderful, way. What does this say to you about God's "works" and God's "thoughts"?

God Is Your Strength

In times of persecution, rejection, and struggle, Psalm 62 has often helped my LGBT friends find some solace, rest, and strength. It can also be a balm to family members and allies who may themselves feel the need for consolation.

> For God alone my soul waits in silence;
>   from him comes my salvation.
> He alone is my rock and my salvation,
>   my fortress; I shall never be shaken.

How long will you assail a person,
  will you batter your victim, all
    of you,
  as you would a leaning wall, a
    tottering fence?
Their only plan is to bring down a
  person of prominence.
    They take pleasure in falsehood;
they bless with their mouths,
  but inwardly they curse.

For God alone my soul waits in silence,
  for my hope is from him.
He alone is my rock and my salvation,
  my fortress; I shall not be shaken.
On God rests my deliverance and my
  honor;
    my mighty rock, my refuge is
      in God.

Trust in him at all times, O people;
  pour out your heart before him;
  God is a refuge for us.

Those of low estate are but a breath,
  those of high estate are a
    delusion;
in the balances they go up;
  they are together lighter than a
    breath.
Put no confidence in extortion,
  and set no vain hopes on robbery;
  if riches increase, do not set your
    heart on them.

Once God has spoken;
  twice have I heard this:
that power belongs to God,

and steadfast love belongs to you,
    O Lord.
For you repay to all
    according to their work.

Reflection Questions

1. What image appeals most to you in this psalm: God as *salvation, rock, fortress,* or *refuge*? Why?

2. As you look back over your life, in what ways has God been your "strength"?

3. What does it mean to "pour out" your heart to God? Can you do that now in prayer, confident that God hears you?

4. *For families, friends, and allies:* The process of accepting the sexuality of a family member or friend can be challenging. In what ways has God been your rock? How can God be a rock for you in the future?

Jesus Proclaims His Identity

When Jesus entered the synagogue in Nazareth to preach from the Hebrew Scriptures and announce his identity and mission,
he probably knew how his fellow townspeople
would respond. After all, he had lived among
them in the small town of Nazareth (only two
to four hundred people in Jesus's time) for thirty
years. Despite that, he boldly proclaims who he
is and what he stands for.

Many LGBT people have told me that this passage has helped them own their identity in the face of misunderstanding and opposition, even from those closest to them. And make no mistake: the townspeople are furious at Jesus, going so far as to attempt to "hurl him off the cliff." Knowing of their probable reaction, Jesus says what he needs to say anyway. The passage is often called the "Rejection at Nazareth," but I like to think of it as the "Proclamation of Jesus's Identity."

> When he came to Nazareth, where he had been brought up, he went to the synagogue on the sabbath day, as was his custom. He stood up to read, and the scroll of the prophet Isaiah was given to him. He unrolled the scroll and found the place where it was written:
>
> "The Spirit of the Lord is upon me,
>> because he has anointed me
>>> to bring good news to the poor.

He has sent me to proclaim release to
   the captives
         and recovery of sight to the blind,
               to let the oppressed go free,
to proclaim the year of the Lord's favor."

And he rolled up the scroll, gave it
back to the attendant, and sat down.
The eyes of all in the synagogue were
fixed on him. Then he began to say to
them, "Today this scripture has been
fulfilled in your hearing." All spoke
well of him and were amazed at the
gracious words that came from his
mouth. They said, "Is not this Joseph's
son?" He said to them, "Doubtless
you will quote to me this proverb,
'Doctor, cure yourself!' And you will
say, 'Do here also in your hometown
the things that we have heard you did
at Capernaum.' " And he said, "Truly
I tell you, no prophet is accepted in
the prophet's hometown. But the

truth is, there were many widows in Israel in the time of Elijah, when the heaven was shut up three years and six months, and there was a severe famine over all the land; yet Elijah was sent to none of them except to a widow at Zarephath in Sidon. There were also many lepers in Israel in the time of the prophet Elisha, and none of them was cleansed except Naaman the Syrian." When they heard this, all in the synagogue were filled with rage. They got up, drove him out of the town, and led him to the brow of the hill on which their town was built, so that they might hurl him off the cliff. But he passed through the midst of them and went on his way. (Luke 4:16–30)

Reflection Questions

1. Do you think it was difficult for Jesus to proclaim his identity in front of people who knew him so well?

2. What do you think enabled Jesus to do this? What enables you to accept yourself as you are?

3. Jesus faced fierce opposition both here in his hometown and, later in his ministry, elsewhere. Opposition from those closest to us can be painful. Can you speak to Jesus about that pain? Can you let him speak to you?

4. After this rejection at Nazareth, Jesus finds people who are eager to hear his word in the towns and villages around the Sea of Galilee. What have been your places of rejection and acceptance?

5. Jesus knows what it is like to be rejected. How does this make you feel toward him? Can you share that with him in prayer?

6. *For families, friends, and allies:* What was it like for you when your family member or friend first shared his or her sexuality with you? Have you ever known people who wanted to, figuratively, hurl that person off a cliff? What was your reaction?

Jesus Calls Peter

Sometimes we doubt that we are "worthy" of following Jesus or being loved by God. All of us—straight, gay, lesbian, bisexual, transgender—are imperfect. All of us have our flaws. All of us sin. Yet God calls all of us. Peter's response is typical—aware of our sinfulness, we feel unworthy in the face of God's call and unworthy of God's generosity. Jesus calls us anyway.

Once while Jesus was standing beside the lake of Gennesaret, and the crowd

was pressing in on him to hear the word of God, he saw two boats there at the shore of the lake; the fishermen had gone out of them and were washing their nets. He got into one of the boats, the one belonging to Simon, and asked him to put out a little way from the shore. Then he sat down and taught the crowds from the boat. When he had finished speaking, he said to Simon, "Put out into the deep water and let down your nets for a catch." Simon answered, "Master, we have worked all night long but have caught nothing. Yet if you say so, I will let down the nets." When they had done this, they caught so many fish that their nets were beginning to break. So they signaled their partners in the other boat to come and help them. And they came and filled both boats, so that they began to sink. But when Simon Peter saw it, he fell down at Jesus' knees, saying, "Go away from me, Lord, for I am a sinful man!" For he and all who were with him were amazed at the catch of fish that they had taken; and so also were James and John, sons of Zebedee, who were partners with Simon. Then Jesus said to Simon, "Do not be afraid; from now on you will be catching people." When they had brought their boats to shore, they left everything and followed him. (Luke 5:1–11)

Reflection Questions

1. In the face of the divine, Peter naturally feels his imperfections. Bill Creed, a Jesuit spiritual director, once described this common experience by saying, "In the sunshine of God's love, we see our shadows." What are the "shadows" in your life? Can you bring them before God in prayer, as Peter does here?

2. Nets bursting with fish is a powerful image of the abundance of blessings that God has given us. This abundance enables Peter to trust in Jesus. If you were to list your blessings, what would be in your "net"?

3. Peter says he had worked all night and caught nothing. Without Jesus, we can do nothing. With him, we can do everything. Where could you use Jesus's help? Can you ask for it in prayer?

4. *For families, friends, and allies:* You have many "calls" in your life. One is to love your family members and friends in all their complexity. But sometimes you might feel inadequate to the task, as Peter did. What helps you love and support your LGBT family members and friends? What "catch of fish" encourages you?

The Risen Christ Appears to Mary Magdalene

Things often seem hopeless. In fact, after the Crucifixion, for the remainder of Good Friday and all of Holy Saturday, the disciples were bereft. And frightened. They wondered if the same fate that had befallen their leader would happen to them. Their hope for the world seemed to be gone. But the Resurrection shows that love always triumphs over hatred, life triumphs over death, and hope triumphs over despair.

By the way, notice that it was not to one of the "inner circle," that is, the twelve men, to whom the newly resurrected Jesus appeared first, but to a woman. In the Gospel of John, it is Mary Magdalene, not Peter, who is first tasked with announcing the Good News.

Indeed, for the space of time—minutes or hours—between when the Risen Christ appeared to her and when she announced the Resurrection to the disciples, Mary Magdalene *was* the church on earth: she alone understood the mystery of Jesus's life, death, and resurrection.

It's another reminder of God's love for those often seen as "less than" by the rest of the world.

> **Early on the first day of the week,
> while it was still dark, Mary Magdalene
> came to the tomb and saw that the
> stone had been removed from the tomb.
> So she ran and went to Simon Peter**

and the other disciple, the one whom Jesus loved, and said to them, "They have taken the Lord out of the tomb, and we do not know where they have laid him." Then Peter and the other disciple set out and went toward the tomb. The two were running together, but the other disciple outran Peter and reached the tomb first. He bent down to look in and saw the linen wrappings lying there, but he did not go in. Then Simon Peter came, following him, and went into the tomb. He saw the linen wrappings lying there, and the cloth that had been on Jesus' head, not lying with the linen wrappings but rolled up in a place by itself. Then the other disciple, who reached the tomb first, also went in, and he saw and believed; for as yet they did not understand the scripture, that he must rise from the dead. Then the disciples returned to their homes.

But Mary stood weeping outside the tomb. As she wept, she bent over to look into the tomb; and she saw two angels in white, sitting where the body of Jesus had been lying, one at the head and the other at the feet. They said to her, "Woman, why are you weeping?" She said to them, "They have taken away my Lord, and I do not know where they have laid him." When she had said this, she turned around and saw Jesus standing there, but she did not know that it was Jesus. Jesus said to her, "Woman, why are you weeping? Whom are you looking for?" Supposing him to be the gardener, she said to him, "Sir, if you have carried him away, tell me where you have laid him, and I will take him away." Jesus said to her, "Mary!" She turned and said to him in Hebrew, "Rabbouni!" (which means Teacher). Jesus said to her, "Do not hold on to me, because I have not yet ascended to the

Father. But go to my brothers and say to them, 'I am ascending to my Father and your Father, to my God and your God.'" Mary Magdalene went and announced to the disciples, "I have seen the Lord"; and she told them that he had said these things to her. (John 20:1–18)

Reflection Questions

1. Can you remember a time that seemed hopeless? What helped you move ahead?

2. What gives you hope? Where have been your "resurrections"?

3. Who gives you hope? Who announces the Good News to you? Who is your Mary Magdalene? And to whom do you announce the Good News?

4. For a time, Mary Magdalene was the church on earth. If you had to name one

person who was the church for you in a dark time, who would it be?

5. Can you thank God for the grace of hope?

6. *For families, friends, and allies:* Where have you found signs of the Resurrection in the lives of your LGBT family members and friends? Where do you see it in the church?

The Road to Emmaus

Often things seem hard to understand, comprehend, or accept. That's the case for all of us at different points in our lives. The story of the two despairing disciples walking away from Jerusalem shows us what happens when we allow God to open our eyes to a new way, when we allow ourselves to reflect on what God has been doing, and when we find God in the midst of community.

Now on that same day two of them were going to a village called Emmaus, about seven miles from Jerusalem, and talking with each other about all these things that had happened. While they were talking and discussing, Jesus himself came near and went with them, but their eyes were kept from recognizing him. And he said to them, "What are you discussing with each other while you walk along?" They stood still, looking sad. Then one of them, whose name was Cleopas, answered him, "Are you the only stranger in Jerusalem who does not know the things that have taken place there in these days?" He asked them, "What things?" They replied, "The things about Jesus of Nazareth, who was a prophet mighty in deed and word before God and all the people, and how our chief priests and leaders handed him over to be condemned to death and crucified him. But we had hoped that he was the one to redeem Israel. Yes, and besides all this, it is now the third day since these things took place. Moreover, some women of our group astounded us. They were at the tomb early this morning, and when they did not find his body there, they came back and told us that they had indeed seen a vision of angels who said that he was alive. Some of those who were with us went to the tomb and found it just as the women had said; but they did not see him." Then he said to them, "Oh, how foolish you are, and how slow of heart to believe all that the prophets have declared! Was it not necessary that the Messiah should suffer these things and then enter into his glory?" Then beginning with Moses and all the prophets, he interpreted to them the things about himself in all the scriptures.

As they came near the village to
which they were going, he walked
ahead as if he were going on. But
they urged him strongly, saying, "Stay
with us, because it is almost evening
and the day is now nearly over." So
he went in to stay with them. When
he was at the table with them, he
took bread, blessed and broke it, and
gave it to them. Then their eyes were
opened, and they recognized him; and
he vanished from their sight. They
said to each other, "Were not our
hearts burning within us while he was
talking to us on the road, while he was
opening the scriptures to us?" That
same hour they got up and returned
to Jerusalem; and they found the
eleven and their companions gathered
together. They were saying, "The Lord
has risen indeed, and he has appeared
to Simon!" Then they told what had

happened on the road, and how he had been made known to them in the breaking of the bread. (Luke 24:13–35)

Reflection Questions

1. When were your eyes "kept from recognizing" God? What prevented you from seeing God in these moments?

2. What enables you to notice the presence of God in difficult times?

3. If you told the story of your own "Road to Emmaus," what would that story be?

4. *For families, friends, and allies:* At various points in your life, your eyes may also have been "kept from recognizing" the presence of God's grace in the life of your family member or friend. What opened your eyes?

A Prayer for
When I Feel
Rejected

The rash of suicides among LGBT youths cannot fail to move the Christian heart, or indeed any heart capable of compassion. Although any suicide is a terrible tragedy, the suicide of a young person who feels that his or her life will never change, and who moves toward despair as a result of bullying and harassment, seems especially poignant.

Many gays and lesbians, young and old, have told me how wounded they have felt by their churches and other religious organizations. Churches are invited to find a way to reach out more compassionately to LGBT youths, to help them feel valued and know that they are beloved by God—and by us. We must lead as Jesus did, first with welcome, not condemnation.

For my part, here is a prayer composed for all who feel excluded, rejected, marginalized, shamed, or persecuted, in any way or in any place, religious or otherwise.

A Prayer for When
I Feel Rejected

Loving God,
you made me who I am.
I praise you and I love you, for I am
   wonderfully made,
in your own image.
But when people make fun of me,
I feel hurt and embarrassed and even ashamed.
So please, God, help me remember my own
   goodness,

which lies in you.
Help me remember my dignity,
which you gave me when I was conceived.
Help me remember that I can live a life of love,
because you created my heart.

Be with me when people make me feel
   "less than,"
and help me to respond the way you would
   want me to,
with a love that respects the other, but also
   respects me.
Help me find friends who love me for who I am.
Help me, most of all, to be a loving person.

And, God, help me remember that Jesus loves me.
For he too was seen as an outcast.
He too was misunderstood.
He too was beaten and spat upon.
Jesus understands me and loves me with a
   special love,
because of the way you made me.

And when I am feeling lonely,
help me remember that Jesus welcomed everyone as
    a friend.
Jesus reminded everyone that God loved them.
Jesus encouraged everyone to embrace their dignity,
even when others were blind to that dignity.
Jesus loved everyone with the love that you
    gave him.
And he loves me too.

One more thing, God:
Help me remember that nothing is impossible
    with you,
that you have a way of making things better,
that you can find a way of love for me,
even if I can't see it right now.
Help me remember all these things in the heart
    you created,
loving God.

Amen.

ACKNOWLEDGMENTS

Many people contributed to the writing of this book, and I am grateful to them.

First, I would like to thank New Ways Ministry for inviting me to deliver the lecture upon which this book is based, especially Sister Jeannine Gramick, SL, and Frank De Bernardo. I would like to thank John Cecero, SJ, and Robert Hussey, SJ, the Jesuit Provincials of the USA Northeast and Maryland Provinces of the Society of Jesus, respectively, and Matt Malone, SJ, editor in chief of America Media, for their support of the original address and this book.

Thanks also to my Jesuit brothers, of all ages, who have supported me in my informal ministry to the LGBT community over these many years. I am far from the only Jesuit who engages in this kind of ministry.

Also, I would like to thank James Alison, James F. Keenan, SJ, Michael O'Loughlin, Arthur Fitzmaurice, and Dan De Brakeleer for their comments on both the talk and the manuscript. Thanks to Joseph McAuley at *America* for his careful fact-checking. Thanks to Mickey Maudlin, Mark Tauber, Anna Paustenbach, Noël Chrisman, Ann Moru, and Adia Colar of HarperOne for their careful edits, suggestions, and support of this book. Thanks to Adrian Morgan for an eye-catching cover. Finally, I'd like to thank Ivan and Marcos Uberti for their friendship and support.

Most of all, I want to thank the many LGBT Catholics who have shared their experiences of the ways God has been at work in their lives. They have shown me what it means to be "wonderfully made."